The Unofficial F.R.I.E.N.D.S Recipe Book

Delicious Recipes from Everyone's Favorite Show!

Table of Contents

Introduction

Looking for fun recipes to try out? Kind of, sort of obsessed with the classic FRIENDS show? So what happens when you combine the two? Delicious FRIENDS based recipes! If you're as excited as we are, then continue reading for recipes on some classics like the "Chanberry sauce" or Joey's Italian sub!

These recipes have been compiled to make by even the more beginner cooks and are simple yet delicious and filling. So let's not waste time any longer and get started!

Recipes

1. The one with the Hummus attack

Looking for a quick snack? Try out this delicious Hummus! Just make sure not to hurl it at your friends right before an award ceremony and you're good to go!

Total Time: 25m

Serves: 4

Ingredients:

- 1 8 oz. tin chickpeas, drained
- 2 tbsp. water
- ½ clove garlic

- Juice of ½ a small lemon
- 1 tbsp. tahini
- 1 tbsp. extra virgin olive oil
- Salt and pepper

Instructions:

2. To make the hummus, add all the ingredients except the salt and pepper into a blender and process till smooth.

3. Season with salt and pepper as needed.

4. Taste and add in more lemon juice if needed.

5. You can adjust the thickness with a little water to your desired consistency!

6. Serve with pita bread and veggie sticks. Enjoy!

2. The one with the Onion Tartlets

While you'll need to wait more than 6 and half minutes for these delicious tartlets, they're completely worth it!

Total Time: 1h 5m

Makes: 20 tartlets

Ingredients:

- 2 tsp olive oil
- 2 small red onions, thinly sliced
- 2 small yellow onions, thinly sliced
- 1 tbsp. white balsamic vinegar
- 1 sheet frozen puff pastry dough, thawed
- 1/3 cup shredded cheddar cheese

- 1/4 tsp. salt

Instructions:

1. In a skillet, heat oil over med-high heat. Add in the onions and cook for about 5 minutes before reducing heat to medium. Cook for an additional 15 minutes. Add in the vinegar.

2. Preheat oven to 400 F.

3. Lightly dust your work surface with flour before rolling out the dough. Roll into a 10 x 9 inch rectangle and cut into 20 smaller rectangles.

4. Lightly score each piece about 1/8 inch from the edge and prick the surface with a fork to create air gaps.

5. Lay the pieces out on a baking sheet lined with baking paper. Allow to rest for 10 minutes.

6. To prepare the tartlets, sprinkle on about ¾ tsp of cheese on each piece of dough and top with 1 tbsp. of the onion mixture. Sprinkle with salt and bake for 15 minutes or until lightly browned.

7. Serve as an appetizer or a delicious snack!

3. The one with Rachel's Side Salad

Rude waitress aside, this delicious side salad is quick and easy to toss together!

Total Time: 10m

Makes: 1 cup

Ingredients:

- 4 oz. grilled chicken breast, cut into thin strips
- 2 cups chopped lettuce

- 1/3 cup julienned carrots
- 1/3 cup chopped cucumber
- 1/4 cup chopped red onion
- 1 oz. crumbled goat cheese
- Raspberry vinegar to taste

Instructions:

1. In a salad bowl, combine all the ingredients together and toss to mix through.

2. Adjust the raspberry vinegar to taste before tossing again

3. Serve cold!

4. The one with the Free Crab Cakes

Been stood up? These delicious crab cakes are here to save the day!

Total Time: 10m

Makes: 4 servings

Ingredients:

Crab Cake -

- 1 lb. lump crab meat
- 1/2 cup chopped bell pepper

- 2 large eggs, separated
- 2 tsp Old Bay Seasonings
- 2 tbsp. mayonnaise
- 1 clove garlic, minced
- 1 tbsp. chopped fresh cilantro
- Seasoning to taste
- 1/4 cup cornstarch
- 1 tbsp. olive oil
- Panko bread crumbs

Sauce -

- 1 cup mayonnaise
- 4 cloves garlic, crushed
- 1 tbsp. fresh herbs
- 1 tbsp. fresh lemon juice
- Salt to taste

Instructions:

1. In a medium bowl, combine all the sauce ingredients and mix until smooth. Chill covered until required.

2. Prepare the crab mixtures by combining the crab meat, one beaten egg, bell peppers, Old Bay seasoning, mayo, garlic, cilantro salt and pepper. Fold gently until well combined.

3. Chill for at least 1 hours and up to 5 hours.

4. Beat the other egg in a shallow dish. Place the breadcrumbs in a separate dish.

5. Divide the crab cake mixture into 8 balls and flatten each to form a disc about 3 inches in diameter.

6. Lay on a tray and sprinkle the crab cakes with a little bit of cornstarch.

7. One at a time, dip each cake into the egg and then the breadcrumbs, doing this with all the crab cakes.

8. Heat olive oil in a large pan over medium heat. Once hot, start frying the crab cakes for about 3-4 minutes on each side until golden brown.

9. Serve warm with prepared sauce and enjoy!

5. The one with the Unagi Rolls

Maybe you have Unagi, maybe you don't. With these delicious recipe, you can certainly have the food version of it! Unagi refers to Eel but don't let that throw you off. These rolls are delicious and work well with a Sushi spread!

Total Time: 30m

Makes: 4 servings

Ingredients:

Eel sauce –

- 6 tbsp. soy sauce

- 4 tbsp. mirin
- 2 tbsp. brown sugar
- dash of rice wine vinegar

Unagi Rolls -

- 4 cups cooked sushi rice (season to taste)
- 1 package nori sheets
- 1/2 lb. salmon, sliced into 1/2-inch thick strips
- 1 lb. eel, sliced into 1-inch strips
- 8 tbsp. masago
- 1 ripe avocado, peeled and cut into thin slices

Garnish and condiments -

- Toasted sesame seeds
- Wasabi
- Soy sauce
- Pickled ginger

Instructions:

1. To make the eel sauce, combine all the ingredients in a small pan and bring to boil. Boil for 1-2 minutes and then reduce to a simmer until slightly thickened. Remove from heat and allow to cool.

2. To make the rolls, lay out one sheet of nori on a sheet of plastic wrap. Wet your hands and grab a handful of rice and spread across the top 2/3rds of the nori sheet. Press down to ensure the rice sticks to the seaweed.

3. Flip the sheet over so the rice now touches the plastic wrap. Spread the salmon, avocado and masago on the bottom 1/3rd of the nori ensuring you leave a little space on each end.

4. Using the plastic wrap to help, start to roll from the fillings side upwards and continue rolling until the rice covers the roll. You can use a bamboo mat if you've got one to help you shape the roll and make it compact.

5. Once rolled, remove the bamboo mat and the plastic wrap.

6. Heat up the eel in an oven until warm and place a single layer onto the roll, using plastic to stick together. Remove plastic wrap and brush the top of the eel with the eel sauce and garnish with the sesame seeds.

7. Cut into eat even pieces and serve with your favorite condiments!

6. The one with Monica's Rock Shrimp Ravioli

This ravioli recipe is so delicious it could land you a job as head chef!

Total Time: 45m

Makes: 16 servings

Ingredients:

- 1 package mushroom ravioli
- 1 tbsp. olive oil
- 2 cloves garlic, crushed
- 1 cup white wine

- ½ stick butter
- ½ lb. rock shrimp
- ½ lb. bay scallops
- Salt and Pepper
- Bay leaves

Instructions:

1. In a large pot, bring water to a boil. Once boiling, add in the mushroom ravioli and cook until barely al dente. Remove from heat, drain pasta and reserve ¼ cup of pasta water.

2. As pasta cooks, heat olive oil in a pan. Add in crushed garlic cloves and allow to cook for 1 minute before adding in the wine.

3. Bring to a boil and allow the mixture to reduce for 5 minutes.

4. Add in the butter and season according to taste.

5. Next, add in the shrimp and scallops. Allow to cook for 3 minutes before adding the pasta.

6. Bring a large pot of water to a boil and cook one package of porcini mushroom ravioli* until two minutes before al dente.

7. Meanwhile, heat 1 tbsp. olive oil and 2 whole garlic cloves in a skillet.

8. Add 1 c. white wine and let it reduce by half (about 4-5 minutes).

9. Whisk in 1/2 stick cold butter and season the sauce with salt and pepper.

10. Add in the pasta and the reserved liquid, coating evenly. Cook for another 2 minutes.

11. Serve warm!

7. The one with Chandler's Mac and Cheese

Not up to cooking a big Thanksgiving dinner this year? Or maybe you've got "traumatic family memories" tied to Turkey? This Mac and Cheese is a delicious substitute and can also be made any other time of the year!

Total Time: 35m

Makes: 8

Ingredients:

- 1lb uncooked elbow pasta

- 4 cups grated medium sharp cheddar cheese, divided
- 2 cups grated Gruyere cheese, divided
- ½ cup flour
- 1 stick unsalted butter
- 1 ½ cups whole milk
- 2 ½ cups half and half
- ¼ tsp. paprika
- ½ tbsp. salt
- ½ tsp. black pepper

Instructions:

1. Preheat oven to 325 degrees. Prepare and grease a 9 x 13" baking dish and set aside.

2. Fill a large sauce pan with water. Add in 2 tsp of salt and leave to boil. Once it begins to boil, add in the pasta and cook for a minute less than indicated on the package. Drain and coat with a little bit of olive oil to prevent pasta from sticking.

3. As the pasta cooks, grate the 2 cheeses and combine. Divide the cheese mixture into 4 equal parts (about 1 ½ cups each) – two parts for the sauce, and 2 for layering while baking.

4. In a large saucepan, melt butter over medium heat and sprinkle in the flour. Whisk together until the mixtures looks like wet sand. Cook for 1 minute before slowly pouring in half of the milk and half and half. Whisk until smooth. Slowly pour in the rest of the milk and the half and half and whisk until combined and smooth.

5. Continue cooking until the mixture turns thick and glossy.

6. Add in the spices and 1 ½ cups of the cheese. Wait until the cheese melts before adding in the remaining 1 ½ cups of cheese. Stir together until smooth and melted through.

7. In a large bowl, combine the pasta and the cheese sauce, folding gently to incorporate fully.

8. To bake the pasta, layer half the pasta into the prepared baking dish and top with the 1 ½ cup cheese before finally layering with the rest of the pasta.

9. Top the pasta with the rest of the cheese and bake for 15 minutes and golden brown and bubbly.

10. Serve warm!

8. The one with the Blue nail Quiche

This quiche is an easy and delicious recipe to serve up at a dinner party. Just make sure you don't lose a fingernail in there!

Total Time: 1hr

Makes: 6

Ingredients:

Pastry

- 1 1/3 cup all-purpose flour, plus more to dust
- ¾ stick butter, plus more to grease
- salt

*alternatively use readymade pastry

Filling

- 2 ¼ cup grated cheddar
- 4 tomatoes, sliced
- 1 cup chopped bacon
- 5 large eggs, beaten
- 1/3 cup milk
- 1 cup thick cream
- 2 sprigs fresh thyme
- ground black pepper

Instructions:

1. To make your pastry, sift together the flour and salt in a large bowl. Knead in the butter until the mixture is crumbly.

2. Slowly add in cold water as needed to make the mixture just come together and form a firm dough. Allow to chill for half an hour.

3. Once chilled, lightly flour your work surface. Begin rolling out the pastry until large enough to line a greased 9 inch pan. Allow to chill for another 20 minutes.

4. Preheat the oven to 375 degrees F.

5. Remove pan from the fridge and line the base with baking paper and fill with baking beans. Blind bake for 20 minutes before removing the beans and baking paper and baking for another 5 minutes. Remove from oven and set aside.

6. Reduce oven temperature to 325 degrees F.

7. Fry the bacon pieces until crispy. Set aside.

8. Sprinkle cheese onto the pastry and layer in sliced tomatoes. Add in the fried bacon on top.

9. In a medium bowl, whisk together the eggs, milk, and cream. Season well. Pour over the bacon. Top off with some thyme and finally trim the edges.

10. Bake the quiche for 30-40 minutes or until set. Remove from oven and allow to cool.

11. Cut into wedges and serve warm!

9. The one with the Potatoes 3 ways

Picky eaters or guests with too many demands? Pull a Monica and whip up these delicious potato recipes!

Tater Tots

Total Time: 1h

Makes: 4 dozen tots

Ingredients:

- 2¼ teaspoons salt dissolved in 1 cup water
- 2½ pounds russet potatoes, peeled, cut into inch long pieces.
- 1½ tablespoons all-purpose flour
- ½ teaspoon pepper
- 1 quart peanut or vegetable oil

Instructions:

1. In a food processor, mash together the potatoes and salted water until coarsely ground. Stir occasionally. Pass mixture through a fine mesh until all liquid has been drained out. Discard liquid and transfer potatoes to a large bowl.

2. Microwave for 8-10 minutes until dry and sticky, stirring occasionally. Add in the flour and pepper and mix. Spread potato mixture in an 8 inch square pan lined with aluminum. Freeze until firm. About 50 minutes.

3. Heat oil in a large pan.

4. Take the potato mixture out of the pan and divide into 48 pieces. Fry in 2 batches for 5-7 minutes until golden brown.

5. Serve warm!

Mashed Potatoes with and without lumps

Total Time: 20m

Makes: 4 servings

Ingredients:

- 2 lb. potatoes, peeled, cut into inch long pieces
- Salt and pepper
- ⅔ cup buttermilk, room temperature
- 6 tbsp. unsalted butter, melted

Instructions:

1. Add potatoes to a large pan and pour in 1 inch of cold water. Add in 1 tbsp. salt and bring to boil. Lower heat and simmer until potatoes start to break apart easily, about 15-20 minutes. Drain and return to saucepan.

2. Use a masher and mash potatoes until NO lumps remain. Gently mix buttermilk and melted butter in small bowl until combined. Add buttermilk mixture to potatoes and, using a spatula, gently fold in until just incorporated. Season to taste and serve immediately.

Mashed Potatoes with Lumps

To make the mashed potatoes with lumps, simply cook the potatoes for 3 minutes fewer than required and do not mash too hard. And there you have it!

10. The one with Ross' Spicy Tacos

While tacos may not be Ross's favourite food, these spicy soft tacos are going to be a hit at any gathering! Just be sure to adjust the spice to match your tolerance level!

Total Time: 30m

Makes: 4-6

Ingredients:

- 1 lb. chicken breast, cut into bite sized pieces
- 1 small onion, chopped
- 1 large jalapeno, finely chopped
- 4-6 cloves garlic, minced

- 2 tbsp. olive oil
- 1 tbsp. tomato paste
- 2 tsp chili powder
- 1 tsp cumin
- 1/2 tsp smoked paprika powder
- ½ tsp cayenne pepper
- Salt and pepper to taste
- juice of ½ lime
- flour or corn tortillas

Instructions:

1. In a large skillet, heat the olive oil and add in the onion, pepper, and garlic. Sauté for a 30 seconds before adding in the chicken. Cook until chicken has browned and cooked through.

2. Add in the rest of the ingredients. Cook until chicken has been coated and is dry. To make a saucier filling, add in ¼ cup of water or chicken stock. Set aside

3. Heat up the tortillas and fill with chicken mixture. Serve with your desired toppings!

11. The one with Ross' Fajitas

Remember to use oven gloves when dealing with this fajita recipe! While this Fajita recipe is delicious, maybe try and not invite your ex-girlfriend while making them?

Total Time: 4h 30m

Makes: 8 servings

Ingredients:

Marinade -

- ½ cup olive oil
- 2 limes, juiced
- 6 tbsp. fresh cilantro, finely chopped
- 4 tbsp. onion, thinly sliced
- 6 cloves garlic, minced
- 3 tsp ground cumin
- 2 tsp salt
- 2 tsp black pepper

Fajitas –

- 16 oz. boneless strip steaks, cut into thin slices
- 2 bell peppers, sliced
- 16 6 inch corn tortillas
- 2 8 oz. jar salsa
- 2 8 oz. package shredded Mexican cheese blend

Instructions:

1. In a bowl, mix together marinade ingredients till well combined and then add in the mixture to a plastic sealable

bag. Add in the meat and coat evenly. Allow to marinade for at least 4 hours or overnight.

2. Heat a large skillet over medium heat and cook the bell peppers for 2 minutes before adding in the meat. Cook the beef for 15-20 minutes.

3. Serve the cooked beef with the tortillas, salsa and cheese.

12. The one with the Pizza

This pizza recipe is easy and delicious and you don't even need a pretty delivery girl to bring it to you!

Total Time: 1h 30m

Makes: 1 13 inch pizza

Ingredients:

For the crust:

- 2 cups all-purpose or bread flour, plus more for rolling
- ½ tsp sugar
- 1 1/8 tsp (1/2 envelope) dry yeast

- 1 tsp salt
- ¾ cup water, at 110°F
- 1 tbsp. + 1 tsp, olive oil

For the pizza:

- ½ cup pizza sauce, homemade or store-bought
- 30 slices pepperoni
- 2 cups shredded mozzarella cheese
- ¼ cup parmesan cheese
- 2 tbsp. fresh basil leaves
- Red pepper flakes

Instructions:

1. In the bowl of a stand mixer fixed with the hook attachment, combine the flour, sugar, yeast and salt. With the mixer running, add the water and 1 tablespoon of olive oil and mix until a ball of dough is formed. Add additional flour if the dough seems to be too sticky or add additional water if the dough is too dry.

2. Remove and place the dough on a floured surface and knead for a few minutes into a smooth ball.

3. Grease a large bowl with the remaining olive oil and place the dough in. cover the bowl with plastic wrap and let it rise for about an hour.

4. Preheat the oven to 400°F.

5. After the dough has risen, punch it lightly to deflate. Roll it out to fit your pizza pan. Top evenly with pizza sauce, mozzarella, parmesan and pepperoni. Bake for about 15-20 minutes or until the crust is golden-brown. Sprinkle on the red pepper flakes and serve.

13. The one with Monica's Lasagna

Do like Monica and prepare a lasagna or two to always have as a backup meal! Heat and we're ready to go!

Total Time: 1h 30m

Makes: 12 servings

Ingredients:

- 9 lasagna noodles
- ½ cup water
- 1 pound ground beef
- 1 jar spaghetti sauce

- 32 ounces cottage cheese
- ½ cup grated parmesan, divided
- 3 cups shredded mozzarella cheese, divided
- 2 eggs
- 2 tsp parsley
- salt and ground pepper

Instructions:

1. In a pan, cook off the beef on medium heat and then drain excess grease.

2. Bring back to heat and add in the spaghetti sauce. Cook on low, simmering for 5 minutes until thickened and set aside.

3. To make the cheese mixture, mix the cottage cheese, half of the parmesan, 2 cups of mozzarella cheese, and the eggs. Season with salt and pepper.

4. To make the lasagna, you will need a 9x13 inch dish. Cover the bottom of the dish with ¾ cup of the sauce. Add 3 uncooked lasagna noodles and spread ¾ cup of the cheese mixture.

5. On the cheese mixture add ¼ cup of the beef sauce.

6. Repeat the layers twice, then top with 3 noodles. Spread the remaining sauce, mozzarella and parmesan cheese.

7. To the edges of the dish add ½ cup water. Cover it with aluminum foil and bake for about 45 minutes in a preheated oven at 350 degrees F.

8. Uncover the dish and bake for 10 more minutes. Remove from oven and allow to cool for 15 minutes.

9. Serve hot!

14. The one with Joey's Meatball Sub

Don't share food? No problem. This Joey favorite makes 8 servings making it perfect for a group of friends...or just you!

Total Time: 30m

Makes: 8 servings

Ingredients:

- 1 cup celery, diced
- 1 cup carrots, diced
- 1 cup onion, diced

- 5 cloves garlic, minced
- 1 ½ cups fresh parsley, chopped
- 1 ½ cup bread crumbs
- 1 cup parmesan cheese, divided
- 2 large eggs
- 4 tbsp. ketchup
- Salt and pepper
- 3 lb ground beef
- 8 sandwich rolls, halved lengthwise and toasted
- 2 cups marinara sauce
- 2 cups shredded mozzarella cheese

Instructions:

1. Preheat the oven to 400°F. Line a baking pan with baking paper and set aside.

2. In a large bowl, combine the diced vegetables, garlic, fresh parsley, breadcrumbs, ½ cup parmesan cheese, eggs and ketchup. Season with salt and pepper. Add the beef and mix again until just combined.

3. Form 1 ½ inch meatballs and place on the baking sheet. Bake for about 20 minutes or until meatballs are browned.

4. In the meantime, heat the marinara sauce in a saucepan until warm. Spoon marinara evenly over the meatballs and top with shredded mozzarella. Place the pan back in the oven for about 3 minutes or until the cheese has melted.

5. Place the meatballs in the toasted rolls and sprinkle evenly with the remaining parmesan cheese.

6. Serve.

15. The one with the Thanksgiving Turkey

Be prepared this thanksgiving with this delicious Turkey recipe! Just don't push your head up the Turkey!

Total Time 3h

Makes: 8 servings

Ingredients:

- 1 stick unsalted butter, melted
- Zest and juice of 1 lemon

- 1 large handful + 1 tsp chopped fresh thyme, divided
- 1 10 lb. fresh turkey
- Salt and pepper
- 1 lemon, halved
- 1 large onion, roughly chopped
- 1 head garlic, halved

Instructions:

16. Preheat oven to 350°F.

17. In a small bowl, combine the melted butter with the zest and juice of 1 lemon and 1 tsp chopped thyme leaves.

18. Remove the giblets, excess fat and any leftover pinfeathers from the turkey and wash the turkey thoroughly. Place the turkey in a large pan and sprinkle the cavity with salt and pepper. Place the bunch of thyme, halved lemon, onion and head of garlic inside the turkey. Brush the butter mixture on the outside of the turkey and sprinkle with pepper and salt.

19. Using kitchen string, tie up the legs of the turkey and tuck the wings under the body.

20. Place the turkey in the oven and roast for about 2 ½ hours or until the juices run clear when you pierce the thigh. Remove the turkey from the pan, place onto a serving tray or cutting board, cover with foil and let it rest for 15 minutes.

21. Slice and serve.

16. The one with the Moist Maker

If you've always wanted to try the legendary moist maker, with this recipe you can! This sandwich is the best use of Thanksgiving leftovers!

Total Time: 5m

Makes: 1 cup

Ingredients:

- 3 slices white bread
- roasted turkey breast, sliced
- stuffing

- cranberry sauce
- Tomato slices
- green leaf lettuce
- gravy

Instructions:

1. Spread a thin layer of gravy on two slices of bread and soak the third slice in the gravy.

2. To begin assembling the sandwich, lay a piece of lettuce on one gravy spread slice of bread. Top with turkey slices and a slice of tomato.

3. Lay the gravy soaked bread on top and pile on some stuffing. Layer on some cranberry sauce and top with the third slide, gravy side down.

4. Toast slightly or eat as is!

Sweet

17. The one with the Chanberry Sauce

This cranberry sauce can be made any time of the year and goes deliciously well over cheesecake or fresh fruits or with Turkey!

Total Time: 20m

Makes: 10 servings

Ingredients:

- 4 cups fresh or frozen cranberries
- 1 cup water
- 2½ cups sugar
- 1½ cups light syrup
- ½ cup lemon juice

Instructions:

1. Combine cranberries, water, corn syrup, and sugar in a saucepan and bring to a boil.

2. Once it starts boiling, lower the heat and simmer for 10-15 minutes or until the cranberries have softened.

3. Add in the lemon juice and cook for an additional 2 minutes.

4. Remove from heat and allow to cool.

5. Serve cold!

18. The one with the Mocklate

Okay so maybe this recipe does have chocolate but let's face it, who in their right minds would want to try out mocklate?! These delicious truffles are a quick and easy recipe and can be serves as faux mocklate! Mock-mocklate? We'll let you decide!

Total Time 1h 50m

Makes: 35 truffles

Ingredients:

- 12 oz. bittersweet chocolate, chopped
- 1/3 C. heavy cream

- 1 tsp vanilla extract
- Cocoa Powder

Instructions:

1. In a medium pan mix together the chocolate and cream on medium heat.

2. Cook, stirring till the chocolate melts and mixture becomes smooth. 3. Remove from the heat and add the flavoring and beat well.

3. Transfer the mixture into a small dish and refrigerate for about 1 1/2-2 hours.

4. Make the balls from the mixture and roll in cocoa powder before serving!

19. The one with the Chocolate Torte

Does Joey share food? No. But does he help himself to others' food? Yes. And we can't blame him. This chocolate torte is gooey, fudgy and yummy!

Total Time: 4h

Makes: 12 servings

Ingredients:

- 1 cup dark chocolate, chopped into pieces
- 1 stick butter, unsalted
- 3/4 cup sugar

- a tsp. of coffee powder
- 1/8 tsp. salt
- 3 eggs
- ½ cup cocoa powder

Filling

- 1 ¼ cup thick cream
- 1 ¾ cup dark chocolate, chopped into pieces
- cocoa powder

Instructions:

1. Preheat oven to 375 degrees F. Line a 9" round pan with baking paper and grease lightly.

2. In a large mixing bowl, melt together butter and chocolate in the microwave in 20 second intervals, stirring frequently. Allow to cool slightly.

3. Add in the salt, sugar, and coffee powder. Mix.

4. Add in the eggs and beat together until smooth.

5. Sprinkle in cocoa and mix until just combined.

6. Carefully move batter into pan and bake for 22-25 minutes.

7. Remove from oven and allow to cool slightly before removing from pan.

8. Allow cake to cool completely before serving.

Filling –

1. While the cake bakes, prepare the filling. In a saucepan, heat cream until bubbles start forming around the edges. Remove from heat and add in the chopped chocolate. Allow to melt for 30 seconds before mixing together until evenly combined. Allow to cool to room temperature.

2. Using only half the ganache, cover the top and sides evenly.

3. Scoop out teaspoon sized bits from the rest of the ganache and leave them to chill for 1 hour on wax paper.

4. Once the ganache bits have hardened, shape them into balls using your hands. Work fast to avoid the balls melting. Roll in cocoa powder and set atop the cake.

5. Serve with ice-cream!

20. The one with the Saltwater Taffy

Ross loves his Taffy and with this recipe now so will you!

Total Time: 1hr

Makes: 50 pieces.

Ingredients:

- 1 cup sugar
- 3/4 cup light corn syrup
- 2/3 cup water
- 1 tbsp. cornstarch

- 2 tbsp. butter
- 3/4 tsp. salt
- 2 drops food coloring
- 2 tsp. vanilla

Instructions:

1. In a deep saucepan, combine all ingredients except the vanilla and food coloring.

2. Cook over medium heat, stirring constantly. Cook until the mixture reads 256 degrees F on a cooking thermometer.

3. Add in the food coloring and mix before stirring in the vanilla. Pour into a buttered 8×8 square pan. Let cool.

4. Once cool, begin pulling the taffy. To do this, lightly butter your hands, grab a handful of taffy and begin stretching until it become quite stiff and lighter in colour. Stretch into long ropes and cut into 1 inch strips.

5. Allow the strips to cool for an hour and then wrap in wax paper or serve directly on wax paper.

21. The one with Joey's Pancakes

Fluffy, light and delicious! These pancakes are quick and easy to make and are sure to delight!

Total Time: 30m

Makes: 6

Ingredients:

- 1 cup all-purpose flour, sifted
- 2 tsp baking powder
- pinch of salt
- 2 tbsp. sugar

- 3/4 cup plus 2 tbsp. milk
- 1 large egg, beaten
- 2 tbsp. unsalted butter, melted
- 1 tsp pure vanilla extract
- oil for cooking

Instructions:

1. In a mixing bowl, mix together flour, sugar, salt, and baking powder.

2. In a different bowl, combine the egg, milk, vanilla, and melted butter together.

3. Pour the wet mixture into the dry ingredients and evenly combine. If the batter is too thick to work with, add in a tablespoon of milk. Set aside for 5-10 minutes.

4. Lightly coat a non-stick pan with oil and drop in ¼ cup of pancake batter. Cook until bubbles start forming on top and then flip and cook until golden brown.

5. Serve warm with your favourite topping!

22. The one with Rachel's Trifle

In charge of making the dessert at Thanksgiving? Just be sure you don't pull a Rachel with this trifle and you'll be good to go!

Total Time: 25m + chill time

Makes: 8-10 servings

Ingredients:

- 3/4 cup raspberry or strawberry jam
- 1 ½ lb. strawberries, stem removed, and cut into 1/4-inch slices
- 12 oz. blueberries
- 12 oz. raspberries
- 16 oz. cream cheese, softened
- 1 ¾ cup confectioners' sugar
- 1 ½ cup cold heavy whipping cream
- 1 tsp. vanilla extract
- 1 (7 oz.) package crisp lady fingers

Instructions:

1. Save a couple of berries to use as garnish.

2. In a large bowl, heat the jam using the microwave for about 60 seconds, or until it turns liquid. Add in the fresh berries and coat evenly. Allow to chill.

3. Meanwhile, whip the heavy cream using an electric mixer or by hand until stiff peaks form. Set aside for use later.

4. In a separate bowl, beat the powdered sugar with the softened cream cheese until they are creamy and smooth.

Add in the vanilla, then beat in the third of the whipped cream. Then use a large rubber spatula to fold in the remaining whipped cream until they are well combined.

5. Cover the bottom of a 9-inch trifle dish or glass bowl with a layer of lady fingers (break into pieces if necessary). Follow with 1/3 of the berry-jam mixture (including 1/3 of the juices), then 1/3 of the cream.

6. Alternate, finishing with the cream cheese mixture on the top

7. Garnish with the reserved whole berries and a fresh mint sprig.

8. Refrigerate for at least 8 hours, or overnight, before serving.

23. The one with Monica's Pumpkin Pie

This Pumpkin Pie makes a recurring occurrence on Thanksgiving and we can see why! Creamy and crispy, you are guaranteed to be asked for second helpings!

Total Time: 1h 20m

Makes: 8-10 servings

Ingredients:

Pastry -

- 1 1/3 cup all-purpose flour
- 1 stick cold butter, cubed
- 3 tbsp. caster sugar
- 1 egg yolk

Filling -

- 2 eggs
- ½ cup caster sugar
- 1 tsp. cinnamon
- ½ tsp. mixed spice
- ½ tsp. ginger
- ¾ cup pumpkin puree, homemade or canned.
- ¾ cup evaporated milk
- Whipped cream, to serve.

Instructions:

1. In a food processor, combine the flour and butter together until the mixture is crumbly. Move to a large bowl and add in caster sugar. Stir together to combine.

2. Add in the egg yolk, 2 tbsp. water and combine until even. Knead with your hands until the pastry comes together, wrap in saran wrap and allow to chill for half an hour.

3. On a lightly dusted work surface, roll out the pastry large enough to line an 8 inch round pan. Poke at the base with a fork and chill for another 20 minutes.

4. Remove pan from the fridge and line the base with baking paper and fill with baking beans. Blind bake for 15 minutes before removing the beans and baking paper and baking for another 8 minutes. Remove from oven and set aside. Reduce oven temperature to 375 degrees F.

5. In the meantime, lightly beat the eggs using a handheld electric beater until pale and light ~ 3 minutes. Gently fold through the spices, pumpkin puree and sugar until evenly combined. Fold in the evaporated milk and pour into pastry crust.

6. Ensure oven is at 375 degrees F. Bake pie for 45-50 minutes or until set. Remove from oven and allow to cool before serving.

7. Cut into wedges and serve lightly warm with some fresh cream!

24. The one with Monica's Candy

Tangy and rich, this orange truffle recipe is super easy to whip up and is the perfect treat for neighbors, colleagues and friends!

Total Time: 1h 20m

Makes: 40 pieces

Ingredients:

Truffle Mixture -

- 1/4 cup unsalted butter
- 3 tbsp. heavy cream
- 4 oz. dark chocolate, chopped
- 2 tbsp. orange juice
- 1 tsp grated orange zest

Coating -

- 4 oz. dark chocolate, chopped
- 1 tbsp. Vegetable oil

Instructions:

1. In a sauce pan, combine the butter and cream and bring to boil over medium-high heat.

2. Remove from heat and add in the rest of the truffle ingredients.

3. Pour mixture into a 9x5 inch loaf pan and chill for about 2 hours.

4. Line a large tray with waxed paper and begin forming balls out of the hardened truffle mixture. Arrange on prepared tray. Allow to chill another half an hour.

5. Meanwhile, in a double boiler, melt together chocolate and oil. Stir until smooth.

6. Remove from heat and allow to cool until lukewarm.

7. Remove truffle from the fridge and begin coating in chocolate mixture, one at a time. Arrange on tray and allow to chill one last time.

8. Serve!

25. The one with the Hallway Cheesecake

Creamy, light and delicious, this cheesecake recipe ensure you never have to eat cheesecake out of a hallway!

Total Time: 1h 45m

Makes: 12-14

Ingredients:

- Butter to grease
- 2 cups plain digestive biscuits, ground to crumbs.
- 1 stick butter, melted

- 1 ¼ lb. cream cheese
- ¾ cup caster sugar
- ½ tbsp. vanilla paste
- 1 ¼ cup whipping cream
- 3 large eggs, beaten

Instructions:

1. Preheat oven at 340 degrees F. Prepare a 9 inch spring form pan by greasing the base.

2. Mix ground digestive biscuits with melted butter until evenly combined. Move into the prepared pan and flatten evenly to form the crush.

3. Bake for 10-15 minutes or until lightly golden. Remove and allow to cool.

4. Reduce temperature to 320 degrees F.

5. In a large bowl, using a whisk, mix the cream cheese with the sugar. Add in the vanilla and cream and beat together. Add in the eggs, one at a time. Pour into cooled biscuit base.

6. Bake for 45min-1hr until set but still has a slight jiggle. Turn off oven and leave oven door open to cool slowly.

7. Once cooled, leave in fridge to set overnight.

8. Serve!

26. The one with Phoebe's Cookies

You don't need to try out a 100 different chocolate chip recipes. With this super secret Nestley Toulouse cookie recipe, you can make delicious cookies every time!

Total Time: 35m

Makes: 6 servings

Ingredients:

- 1 cup chocolate chips
- 1-1/3 cup flour
- ½ tsp soda for baking

- Pinch of salt
- 1 cup butter
- 3/4 cup sugar
- 3/4 cup light brown sugar, firmly packed
- 2 eggs
- 1/2 teaspoon vanilla extract

Instructions:

1. In a medium bowl, combine the flour, cocoa powder, salt, and baking soda. Set this aside.

2. In a large mixing bowl, using a hand held mixer, beat together butter and sugars for three minutes until pale and fluffy. Beat in the eggs one at a time, beating well after each addition.

3. Beat in vanilla, making sure to scrape the sides of the bowl. With the mixer on low, beat in dry ingredients.

4. Stir in the chocolate chips. Wrap dough in plastic wrap and freeze for one hour or until firm.

5. Preheat oven to 375 degrees F. Line a baking tray with baking paper and drop dough by level tablespoons, 2 inches apart.

6. Bake 9 minutes or until just set on top. Cool for one minute then transfer to wire rack and cool completely before serving!

27. The one with Monica's Jam

Tangy, sweet and rich, this homemade jam tops all other jams out there! This recipe makes plenty to go around as well!

Total Time: 35m

Makes: 2 cups

Ingredients:

- 5 cups ripe strawberries, prepared.
- 7 cups sugar
- 1 box fruit pectin

Instructions:

1. To prepare fruit, wash and stem strawberries. Crush in a food processor and transfer to a saucepan.

2. Mix fruit pectin into the strawberries. Cook over high heat and stir together until mixture comes to a full boil. Immediately add in sugar and stir.

3. Bring to a rolling boil and boil for 1 minutes, stirring constantly.

4. Remove from heat and skim off foam using a metal spoon.

5. Ladle the jam into jars and cover tightly.

6. Place jars in a vat of boiling water to process for 5 minutes.

7. Allow to cool and it is ready to use!

28. The one with the Birthday Flan

While most people would prefer cake on their birthdays, if you're looking for something not so traditional, this Flan recipe works wonderfully!

Total Time: 1h 30m

Makes: 6 servings

Ingredients:

- 1 cup sugar, divided
- 1/4 cup water
- 2 cups whole milk
- 4 large eggs

- 1 teaspoon vanilla extract
- Pinch of salt

Instructions:

1. Preheat oven to 350°F. Add 1/2 cup sugar and 1/4 cup water in a small saucepan on low heat. Cook until sugar dissolves. Once dissolved, increase heat and bring the mixture to a boil. Be careful not to stir. Cook until the caramel turns a deep amber color. This should take about 10 minutes. Pour caramel into an 8 inch ceramic dish. Carefully tilt the mixture so it evenly coats the sides as well.

2. In a medium saucepan, combine the milk and 1/2 cup sugar over low heat just until sugar dissolves. In a bowl, whisk the eggs together until well mixed. Carefully pour into the milk mixture, stirring constantly. Whisk in vanilla and salt, then strain into prepared dish.

3. Place dish into a large baking pan. Pour in hot water into the baking pan, allowing the water to come up halfway up the sides of the ceramic dish.

4. Bake flan until the center is just set – about 45-50 minutes. Remove dish from hot water and allow to cool for 30 minutes before chilling in the fridge until cold – about 4

hours or overnight. Using a knife, score along the edges Remove cups from water and let stand 30 minutes. Chill until cold, at least 4 hours and up to 1 day. Cut around sides of each cup to loosen the flan and then turn out onto a flat serving tray.

5. Serve with fresh berries and whipped cream!

29. Bonus Recipe - Central Perk Coffee

Quick and simple, try out this delicious coffee recipe for a quiet afternoon with friends.

Total Time: 1h 40m

Makes: 8 servings

Ingredients:

- 3 tsp instant coffee
- 4 tsp sugar
- 1 ½ cups milk
- ½ water

- Cinnamon, for dusting (optional)

Instructions:

1. Divide instant coffee and sugar evenly between two mugs. Add a teaspoon of milk to each and stir for a minute or until the mixture has lightened.

2. Heat the milk and water in a medium-sized saucepan over medium-high heat for about 3 minutes or until the mixture just starts to boil. Pour evenly into mugs and stir until well combined.

30. Bonus Recipe - Central Perk Muffins

Try out these delicious café style muffins that are perfect to have with a warm cup of fresh coffee!

Total Time: 30m

Makes: 12

Ingredients:

- 2 ½ cup all-purpose flour
- ½ tsp salt
- 1 tbsp. baking powder
- 1 tsp baking soda

- ½ cup unsalted butter, melted
- 1 cup granulated sugar
- 2 large eggs
- 1 cup buttermilk
- 1 tbsp. vanilla extract
- 1 ½ cup semi-sweet chocolate chips

Instructions:

1. Preheat oven to 425°F. Line a 12 cup muffin tray paper liners.

2. In a mixing bowl, combine the dry ingredients and chocolate chips together.

3. In a separate bowl, whisk together the rest of the ingredients. Slowly add in the dry ingredients and fold together gently. DO NOT over mix.

4. Carefully divide the batter into the baking cups and bake for 5 minutes.

5. Reduce temperature to 375 F and continue baking for 12-15 minutes or until cooked through the center.

6. Allow to cool slightly before serving!

Conclusion

And there we have it! 30 delicious and super fun FRIENDS based recipes for you try out! Now when you see these delicious dishes on screen, you've got no excuse to not go ahead and whip them up yourself!

These recipes are also great for FRIENDS themed parties! So go ahead and try out these 30 delicious recipes!